REACHING FOR THE STARS

MICHAEL JACKSON
Music's Living Legend

by Rosemary Wallner

Published by Abdo & Daughters, 6535 Cecilia Circle, Edina, Minnesota 55439.

Library bound edition distributed by Rockbottom Books, Pentagon Tower, P.O. Box 36036, Minneapolis, MN 55435.

Library of Congress Number: 91-073036   ISBN: 1-56239-057-0

Cover photo: Pictorial Parade
Inside photos: Retna Ltd: 4, 15, 27, 29, 31; Pictorial Parade: 8, 13, 19, 21

Edited by Bob Italia

TABLE OF CONTENTS

A SUPERSTAR

Since the early 1960s, fans have enjoyed the music of Michael Jackson. Millions of people have seen him grow up on stage. They've seen him progress from the seven-year-old lead singer of the Jackson Five to a successful solo recording artist.

He's been nicknamed "The World's Greatest Entertainer" and has put out hit album after hit album. But his talent goes beyond writing and performing songs. In the early 1980s, he almost single-handedly pioneered the making of music videos. By 1991, with more than a dozen number-one singles to his credit, he signed another record deal while pursuing his other great love: acting.

From New York to California, from countries around the globe, fans have come to know and love the magic of Michael Jackson.

Michael Jackson entertains his audiences with all types of song and dance moves.

1958-1968:
A MUSIC CAREER BEGINS

Michael Joseph Jackson was born on August 29, 1958, to Joseph and Katherine Jackson. He was the seventh of nine children. His older brothers and sisters are Maureen ("Rebbie"), Jackie, Tito, Jermaine, LaToya, and Marlon. His brother Randy and sister Janet were born a few years later.

The Jacksons lived on Jackson Street in Gary, Indiana. Their house had only three bedrooms, so there wasn't much privacy–but there was music.

Both of Jackson's parents loved music. When Joe Jackson saw that his children were also interested in music, he decided to form a family band. He bought second-hand instruments for his children and began to teach them everything he knew about playing and singing. Tito and Jackie played guitar, Jermaine played bass and sang lead vocals, and Maureen and LaToya played violin and clarinet. Michael, who was not yet four years old, watched his brothers and sisters constantly.

Maureen and LaToya soon lost interest in the group, but their brother Marlon joined when he was six years old and filled the gap. One day, Katherine Jackson saw Michael imitating Jermaine and playing the bongo drums. Michael sang so well that, at age five, his brothers made him the lead singer of their group. A neighbor called them the Jackson Five and the name stuck.

The Jacksons spent much of their after-school time rehearsing. Soon they began to enter–and win–talent contests throughout Indiana and Illinois. Jackson's father quit his job to become the group's manager.

The Jackson Five performed for more and larger audiences in Chicago and New York.They began to open for well-known performers like Gladys Knight and the Pips.

"While my brothers and I were. . .opening for other acts," remembered Jackson, "I carefully watched all the stars because I wanted to learn as much as I could."

The Jackson Five's big break came in 1969 when eleven-year-old Jackson and his brothers auditioned for Motown Records in Detroit, Michigan. At the time, Motown was the recording studio for some of the hottest black musical talent. Berry Gordy, Motown's president, signed them up. The Jackson Five were on their way to success.

In the early 1970s, Michael posed with his two biggest fans – his mother and father.

1969-1975:
THE MOTOWN YEARS

After the Jackson's signed with Motown, the whole family moved to Los Angeles, California, where Motown's recording studios were now located.

"When we flew to California from Chicago," said Jackson. "It was like being in another country, another world. To come from our part of Indiana, which is so urban and often bleak, and to land in Southern California was like having the world transformed into a wonderful dream."

Motown executives worked with the Jacksons to improve their look. They ordered new costumes, updated hairstyles, and taught the young performers more modern and unique dance steps. They coached them on how to answer interview questions and how to act professionally. Finally, Berry Gordy felt the boys were ready to make their debut.

In November 1969, the single "I Want You Back" was released. Early the next year, the Jackson Five performed on the "Ed Sullivan Show." The TV audience loved the group, but they were especially impressed with young Michael's amazing voice and dance steps.

The rest of 1970 was filled with success. The group's first album, *Diana Ross Presents The Jackson Five*, was released as was their popular single "ABC." That single was number one on the record charts by March and won the group their first Grammy Award.

Throughout the 1970s, the Jackson Five toured all across the United States and were interviewed by all the major magazines. Michael, along with his brothers, quickly learned that being famous has its price. The Jacksons rarely went anywhere alone. A bodyguard was always nearby. Michael began to change, also. When the group first formed, he was an energetic, outgoing person. Gradually, Michael found it harder and harder to cope with fans, strangers, and the outside world. He only felt safe at home and on stage.

By 1975, the Jackson brothers were growing up but Motown kept their music the same. The Jackson's father thought that his sons could revitalize their career if they were allowed to write and produce their own songs. When Motown refused, the Jackson Five decided to sign with another record company.

1976-1981: CBS RECORDS

The Jackson Five signed with CBS Records in the spring of 1976 and began to record on the Epic label. Motown executives insisted that their company owned the name "Jackson Five," so the group shortened their name to "The Jacksons."

Over the next three years, The Jacksons worked to improve their music. Michael's popularity grew and he became the newest teenage "heartthrob." Every move he made was reported to his fans. "I may want to go walking or sit in a tree," he said, "but everything we do is on the TV or in the newspapers."

The only time he did leave his home was to go to the recording studio. In 1976 the group's album *The Jacksons* was released. A year later, *Goin' Places* was made. Working with Epic records, the Jacksons wrote and produced more songs. Then Michael was given his first movie role; he was asked to play the scarecrow in the movie version of *The Wiz*.

Jackson was excited about his first movie role. He moved to New York and began work on the movie. *The Wiz*, a black, urban version of *The Wizard of Oz*, starred his friend Diana Ross as Dorothy. Jackson spent four hours each day getting made up with layers of makeup and a wig made of steel wool pads.

"Making *The Wiz* was an education for me on so many levels," said Jackson. "As a recording artist I already felt like an old pro, but the film world was completely new to me. I watched as closely as I could and learned a lot."

The Wiz was released in 1978 and critics praised Jackson for his role as the lovable scarecrow. Jackson had been bitten by the acting bug, and he would continue to look for other movie roles, although his first love was still singing.

In 1979, the Jacksons celebrated ten years in the music business. That same year, twenty-one-year-old Jackson decided to record a solo album. He wasn't splitting from The Jacksons, he assured his fans. He just wanted a chance to see what he could do on his own. Jackson teamed with record producer Quincy Jones to create *Off The Wall*. The album quickly climbed into the Top Ten on the album chart and stayed there for almost eight months.

By 1980, four singles from *Off The Wall* ("Don't Stop 'Til You Get Enough," "Rock With You," "Off The Wall," and "She's Out of My Life") had reached the Top Ten on the singles chart. Jackson had made music history by being the first recording star to produce four Top Ten hits from one album.

*The Jackson Five–Michael (left), Tito, Randy, Jackie, and Marlon–joined
CBS Records in 1976 and became The Jacksons.*

In 1981, The Jacksons went on tour again to promote their newest Epic album, *Destiny*. When the tour ended, Jackson announced that the tour would be his last. And even though there was no official announcement, Jackson decided to pursue his own musical career.

1982-1983: ON HIS OWN

When Jackson decided to become a solo artist, he also decided to change his looks. He had plastic surgery to make his nose thinner, and he began to wear sequined jackets, white socks, and shorter pants. He also began to wear one glove.

"Wearing two gloves seemed so ordinary, but a single glove was different and was definitely a look," explained Jackson. "It's so show business that one glove. I love wearing it."

One of his first projects as a solo artist was to record two duets with Paul McCartney, a former member of the Beatles and head of his own band Wings. The two recorded "Say, Say, Say" and "The Man," both of which appeared on McCartney's album. In return, the two recorded "The Girl is Mine" for Jackson's next album, *Thriller*.

In the early 1980s, Michael began to record on his own; he also decided to change his image. His new look included sequined jackets, white socks, and shorter pants.

When *Thriller* was released in late 1982, it became an instant hit. Jackson had again worked with Quincy Jones to create an album that by March 1983 had reached number one on the charts. The album's singles were becoming just as popular. "Thriller" and "Billie Jean" were the first two singles to be released. "Billie Jean" reached number one on the singles chart three weeks later.

"A musician knows hit material," said Jackson. "It has to feel right. Everything has to feel in place. It fulfills you and it makes you feel good. That's how I felt about 'Billie Jean.' I knew it was going to be big while I was writing it."

Thriller eventually generated seven singles that made it into the Top Ten on the singles chart. Along with "Thriller" and "Billie Jean," "Beat It," "Wanna Be Startin' Something," "PYT (Pretty Young Thing)," "Human Nature," and "The Girl Is Mine" all made it into the Top Ten. The album continued to sell thousands of copies not only in the United States but around the world.

In the midst of his record-breaking success, Jackson found time for another project. The movie *E.T.–The Extra-Terrestrial* had been released in the summer of 1982 and was quickly becoming a hit.

Steven Spielberg, the director of the movie, wanted to produce a storybook album of the movie. When Jackson heard of the idea he was delighted. On the album, Jackson narrates the story and sings the ballad "Someone in the Dark." For Jackson, the best part of making the album was meeting E.T. "He put his arms around me," said Jackson. "He was so real."

About this time, music videos were becoming more popular. Jackson decided to create music videos for the singles "Billie Jean," "Beat It," and "Thriller."

"I was determined to present this music as visually as possible," explained Jackson. "I wanted something that would glue you to the set, something you'd want to watch over and over."

The *Billie Jean* video played on MTV, the rock video cable station in March 1983. The next month, *Beat It*, a video about rival gangs making peace, premiered. In late 1983, Jackson's ghoulish *Thriller* video premiered on the station.

In 1984, Jackson earned a mention in *The Guinness Book Of World Records* when *Thriller* sold over 25 million copies, more than any other album in recording history (since then, it has sold over 40 million copies worldwide). Also that year, the album was nominated for twelve Grammy Awards.

Twenty-five-year-old Jackson attended the awards with actress Brooke Shields and actor Emmanuel Lewis, the child star of the television show *Webster*. That night, Jackson and his producer Quincy Jones made eight trips to the stage to collect their awards. The album *Thriller* won two awards and the single "Thriller" won one. Both "Billie Jean" and "Beat It" won two awards each. Jackson's *E.T.: The Extra-Terrestrial* won for best children's album.

When Jackson received his award for *E.T.*, he told the audience, "Of all the awards I've gotten I'm most proud of this one, honestly. Because I think children are a great inspiration, and this album is not just for children. It's for everyone. I am so happy and so proud. And I just want to say thank you very much."

1984: THE VICTORY TOUR

Despite his success, Jackson still remained close to his family. In mid-1983, Jackson's father asked him to do a 1984 tour with his brothers. Although he didn't like to tour, Jackson agreed.

Jackson was concerned about the quality of the show, however, and made sure that he had control of the tour's dance steps and songs.

At the 1984 Grammy Awards, Michael and producer Quincy Jones collected eight awards for their work on the Thriller *and* E.T. *albums.*

The contract included making two Pepsi commercials and recording a new album.

One commercial shows the four Jacksons in concert with Michael joining his brothers after walking down a set of stairs clouded in colored smoke. The smoke was created with flash powder. During rehearsals, the staff decided they needed more smoke, so they added more flash powder. When Michael walked down the stairs, a flash suddenly erupted. Michael screamed because his hair had caught fire.

An ambulance arrived and rushed Jackson to the burn unit of a nearby hospital. A small circle of burned flesh on the back of Jackson's head was treated, and he was released from the hospital eighteen hours later. Afterwards, he underwent laser surgery to reconstruct the burned spot.

After Jackson's recovery, The Jacksons began recording their album and working out their stage show. At first it was hard for the brothers to work together again. They worked long and hard and by June 1984, their *Victory* album was released.

The Victory Tour began on July 6 in Kansas City, Missouri. Their show was filled with computerized fireworks, red and green lasers, swirling smoke, and other special effects.

In 1984, Michael (far right) and his brothers announce their plans for the Victory Tour to the press.

"It was a nice feeling playing with my brothers again," said Jackson. "It gave us a chance to relive our days as the Jackson Five and The Jacksons. We were all together again."

For all its publicity, Jackson was glad when the tour ended. Recording and touring had taken a full year. Jackson was ready to get on with his own career.

1985-1986: MORE SUCCESSES

In early 1985, Jackson co-wrote "We Are The World" with Lionel Richie. Both men had seen photos of starving children in Ethiopia and the Sudan. They wanted to create a song that would inspire the public to help these people. On January 28, Jackson, Richie, and forty-three other pop music superstars recorded the song in one all-night session.

Within forty-eight hours of its release, the *We Are The World* album sold 500,000 copies. The single earned $8 million for the USA for Africa relief fund. In February 1986, Jackson and Richie accepted four Grammy Awards for the song, including awards for Song of the Year and Best Music Video.

In 1985, the Disney Studios asked Jackson to create a movie for a new ride at Disneyland and Disney World. Jackson, along with directors George Lucas and Francis Ford Coppola, went to work. They created *Captain Eo*, a science-fiction/musical video that used the latest 3-D technologies.

The video's story is about Captain Eo, a young man sent to a faraway planet run by an evil queen. Eo's mission is to bring light and beauty to the planet's inhabitants. "It's a great celebration of good over evil," exclaimed Jackson. The seventeen-minute video premiered on September 12, 1986, at Epcot Center in Florida.

"Working on *Captain Eo* reinforced all the positive feelings I've had about working in film," admitted Jackson, "and made me realize more than ever that movies are where my future path probably lies."

Despite his busy schedule, Jackson found the time to entertain and help needy children. One of his favorite ways to have fun with kids is to invite them to Never Land Ranch, his 2,700-acre home in California.

Never Land Ranch is a huge estate near Santa Barbara, California. It has a twenty-five-room mansion, a zoo, and a private amusement park.

Never Land is also home to Michael's many pets, including a snake named "Muscles." On weekends Jackson invites needy or ill children to visit the many animals that live on the grounds. Many of the children get private tours of his home, also.

The United Negro College Fund (UNCF) is one organization that has also benefited from Jackson's success. In 1983, as the Victory Tour ended, Jackson donated a large portion of his earnings to UNCF. His donations helped to establish the Michael Jackson Scholarship Fund. Since that time, over one hundred scholarships have been given out to students in need.

Jackson remains modest about his contributions. "Performers should always serve as role models who set examples for young people," he said simply.

After *Captain Eo*, Jackson retreated into his studio for the rest of 1985 and all of 1986 and 1987. He kept to himself as he worked on his next album. He wanted this newest album to be as close to perfect as possible. "A perfectionist has to take his time," explained Jackson. "He shapes and he molds and he sculpts that thing until it's perfect. He can't let it go before he's satisfied; he can't."

1987-1989: THE BAD TOUR

The *Bad* album was released on August 31, 1987. Jackson had spent years producing the album; he knew that people were expecting something special.

"[Critics] were waiting to tear me apart when I released my album," said Jackson in early 1989, "but they were soon saying good things about me."

With the release of *Bad* came the start of a sixteen-month world tour to promote the new album. Jackson's Bad Tour began on September 12, 1987, in Japan where 450,000 people saw the first shows. Some fans paid $1,000 for a ticket.

Jackson's first tour without his brothers was a huge undertaking. His crew included 137 professionals: musicians, dancers, technicians, makeup artists, costume preparers, and body guards. The tour equipment filled twelve semi-trailer trucks.

The tour took Jackson and his crew nearly everywhere in the world. He performed 123 concerts in fifteen countries. Over 4 million fans saw his show. In some countries, concerts sold out soon after the tickets went on sale. In other countries sales declined because of bad press about Jackson's eccentric lifestyle.

Throughout the tour, newspapers reported every bit of gossip they could find on Jackson. Some said the star had paid doctors to bleach his skin so it would look whiter. Others said he had his lips thinned. Still others reported he slept in an oxygen tank to stay young and that his closest friend and traveling companion was a chimpanzee named Bubbles. Many tabloids said Jackson wasn't bad, he was weird.

Jackson denied many of these rumors as he crisscrossed the world performing in Australia, Europe, and the United States. The rumors didn't seem to affect the sales of the album. By 1988, five singles from the album ("I Just Can't Stop Loving You," "The Way You Make Me Feel," "Bad," "Man In The Mirror," and "Dirty Diana") had made it to number one on the singles chart. Jackson became the first recording star to score that many number-one hits from one album. By 1989, *Bad* had risen to number one on album charts in twenty-five countries.

The publicity from the tour helped sell more than 20 million albums worldwide. The tour also helped sell copies of Jackson's autobiography *Moonwalk* (titled after the popular backward sliding dance step he popularized) and his video *Moonwalker*.

Michael's Moonwalker *video, released in the late 1980s, is filled with unbelievable dance numbers and special effects.*

On January 27, 1989, in the Los Angeles Sports Arena, thirty-year-old Jackson performed the last concert of the tour. The excitement was high backstage before the concert, but Jackson remained quietly in his dressing room with his sisters and a few close friends.

Seconds before the start of the performance, Jackson came out. He walked the twenty yards to the stage protected by fifteen armed Los Angeles police officers. When he got to the stage, the crowd roared. As 16,000 fans watched, Jackson performed for two energetic hours. After two encores, Jackson triumphantly left the stage. The noise of the fans was deafening.

By the time it was over, the Bad Tour had earned $125 million. Jackson announced that the tour was the last one he would ever do. He assured his fans that he would sing in public again, but he would never travel for such a long time again.

"It has been an incredible experience and I appreciate the power there is in music," explained Jackson in 1989. But the tour had been hard and exhausting and it was time to move on to other projects.

During the Bad Tour, Michael traveled around the world from 1987 to 1989 and performed for over 4 million fans.

THE 1990s: MOVIES AND MORE

In March 1990, CBS Records recognized Jackson for selling 100 million recordings worldwide in the 1980s. *Thriller* and *Bad* had been the two largest-selling albums of the 1980s; nine of his singles had reached the number-one spot. Jackson was officially named the top-selling musical artist of the decade and he showed no signs of slowing down.

In April 1991, he signed one of the largest record deals in history with Sony (who bought CBS Records in 1988). The contract included six new albums, film roles, and bonuses that will reportedly earn Jackson as much as $1 billion. Part of the deal included naming Jackson head of his own record label, which he calls Nation Records. He'll also head the Jackson Entertainment Complex, a company that will oversee the production of films, TV projects, and videos.

But Michael Jackson didn't stop there. His newest album, titled *Dangerous*, promises to be another smash hit.

Michael strives for perfection in whatever he does—whether he's performing on stage, developing a new dance routine, or rehearsing a music video.

What new challenge is ahead for Jackson? He is considering movie deals. "Films can take you anywhere," he explained. "That's what I like. . .so these days movies are my number one dream, but I have a lot of other dreams, too."

Some of Jackson's friends believe that when he does decide on a movie script, the movie will be one that is filled with science fiction and fantasy. But no one knows for sure what this superstar has up his sleeve.

"I think it's so important to set goals for yourself," Jackson declared. "It gives you an idea of where you want to go and how you want to get there. If you don't aim for something, you'll never know whether you could have hit the mark."

MICHAEL JACKSON'S ADDRESS

You can write to Michael Jackson at:

Michael Jackson
4641 Hayvenhurst
Encino, CA 91316

N

FE